THE PIANO

THE PIANO

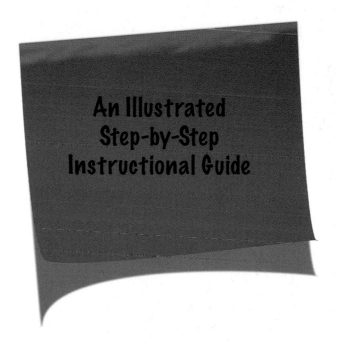

An Illustrated
Step-by-Step
Instructional Guide

Frank Cappelli

ELDORADO INK

Eldorado Ink
PO Box 100097
Pittsburgh, PA 15233
www.eldoradoink.com

CPSIA compliance information: Batch#101909-12. For further information,
contact Eldorado Ink at info@eldoradoink.com.

3 5 7 9 8 6 4

Library of Congress Cataloging-in-Publication Data

Cappelli, Frank.
  The piano / Frank Cappelli.
     p. cm. — (Learn to play)
  Includes bibliographical references and index.
  ISBN-13: 978-1-932904-15-4 (library)
  ISBN-13: 978-1-932904-54-3 (trade)
  1. Piano—Methods. 2. Music theory—Elementary works. I. Title.
  MT224.C29 2007
  786.2'193—dc22

                            2006037089

For information about custom editions, special sales, or premiums,
please contact our special sales department at info@eldoradoink.com.

Acknowledgements

The author would like to thank all of those who provided instruments to
be used in the photographs of this book, particularly Empire Music of
Pittsburgh (412-343-5299; www.empiremusiconline.com).

TABLE OF CONTENTS

Learn to Play

Clarinet
Flute
Guitar
Piano
Trumpet
Violin

INTRODUCTION

The piano is a musical instrument played with a keyboard. When one of the 88 keys is struck, a hammer inside the piano strikes a wire string stretched to a certain tension. This produces the sound of a note.

The idea that tensile strings can be used to produce musical sounds dates to prehistoric times. Perhaps an ancient hunter realized that the string on his bow made a distinct sound when plucked. Eventually, stringed instruments like the harp were developed; the curve of the harp allowed for varied string length, giving each string a different tone.

In the 1300s, an instrument called the harpsichord was developed. As a keyboard instrument that uses strings to create sounds, the harpsichord is an ancestor to our piano. However, unlike a piano, the strings inside a harpsichord are plucked mechanically. Also, at this time a harpsichord player could not increase or decrease the volume of the notes.

In the early 1700s an Italian named Bartolomeo Cristofori invented an instrument he called *gravicèmbalo col piano e forte,* or "harpsichord with soft and loud." (Over time, the instrument's name was shortened to "pianoforte;" it eventually came to be called simply "piano.") In Cristofori's invention the strings were tapped with a little wooden hammer, not plucked. Most importantly, Cristofori invented what is called "escapement," a design that enabled the hammer to strike the string and then rebound to its original position, allowing the strings to vibrate without interference. This gave piano players an opportunity for greater musical expression by varying the volume and duration of the notes they played.

Despite this advantage, it would be many years before the piano was widely accepted. The great composer Johann Sebastian Bach did not approve of the piano until the 1740s. Bach's "The Well-Tempered Clavier," a collection of 48 musical pieces that has been called the Old Testament of piano music, was an important early work. However, it would not be until later in the 18th century, with the success of Wolfgang Amadeus Mozart's piano concertos, that the lasting popularity of the piano was assured.

The piano is a wonderful instrument that can be played in a variety of styles. Anyone can play it, so long as he or she puts in enough time practicing. This book takes a fresh approach to reading music and playing this wonderful instrument. Whether you are a true beginner, have a bit of musical training, or are a skilled musician on another instrument, the approach we have carefully developed can help anyone succeed and continue to enjoy playing the piano. It won't be hard if you practice, so practice a little every day and a lot when you have the time.

In this book I have focused on the most important, interesting, and encouraging part of playing the piano: playing songs. My job is to get you going and hope you find it enjoyable enough to continue to learn and play for years to come.

PART ONE: Getting Started

1. Choosing a Piano

There are two basic types of pianos. Grand pianos (pictured at the top of the opposite page) have their strings and soundboard parallel to the floor, and vertical pianos (or upright pianos, pictured at the bottom opposite) have their strings and soundboard turned perpendicular to the floor. Both of these kinds of pianos are mechanical, and both come in different sizes and styles. Grands can be anywhere from four and one-half feet long to nine and one-half feet long. Uprights can be 52 or more inches high, although there are several smaller types. Studio uprights are around 45 inches tall, consoles are about 40–42 inches, and spinets can be as low as 36–38 inches high.

In the 1960s the electric piano was introduced. This innovation made pianos light enough to easily carry around. Electric pianos used a variety of methods to produce sound. Some used metal reeds that were struck by hammers, some used wire tuning forks, and some used plucked reeds. The mechanically produced sounds were converted into electronic signals. The compact size and relatively inexpensive cost opened the piano to a whole new audience.

More recently the electronic keyboard was developed. It only has electronic parts, and can simulate the sounds of many instruments, including the piano. Electronic keyboards come in a number of grades, with many different options. Professional electronic keyboards can closely mimic the feel and sound of a standard piano for a fraction of the cost.

To start out, go to a music store or a piano store and try the pianos or keyboards. Pick a piano or keyboard that you think looks good or feels good. Pianos are expensive instruments, so if you're going to buy one make sure it's one you will want to play.

In a grand piano (above), the strings and soundboard are parallel to the floor. The keyboard and hammer mechanism of a grand piano are pictured at right. To find the one that's right for you, go to a music store, play the instruments, and ask questions. If you can, go to more than one store.

Compare the way different pianos feel when you press the keys. Some will be easier than others. In a music store the sales people are usually musicians, and they love to talk about music. In most cases they will be happy to help you. For beginners a low-cost electronic keyboard might be the most prudent purchase.

2. The Staff and the Notes

The following will introduce some very basic concepts that will help you to understand the notes on the piano. Music is a language, and it is written on a staff. A staff has five lines and four spaces.

To give order to the music the staff is divided into measures. A vertical line called a bar is used to mark the measures. Here is the staff with a G clef (also called a treble clef), a 4/4 time signature, and a double bar line at the end.

The double bar line tells the piano player that he or she is at the end of a section or strain of music. Sometimes, however, there will be two dots before the double bar line. That means to repeat the section of music.

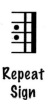

Repeat Sign

The Notes

Next we shall take a look at what gets written on the staff. The notes tell us what tones to play, and take on the names of the lines or spaces they occupy. A note has three parts.

The Head: This gives a general indication of time: a hollow oval indicates a half note or a whole note, while a solid oval denotes a quarter, eighth, or other note.

The Head

The Stem: all notes except for whole notes have a stem.

The Stem

The Flag: the presence of a flag indicates an eighth or sixteenth note.

The Flag

You can find notes *on* the staff, *above* the staff, and *below* the staff.

Quarter Note

Half Note

Eighth Note

A quarter note has a stem and a solid oval head. It usually gets one count. If there are four beats in the measure, you might count "one, two, three, four" in your mind when playing; the quarter note would generally be played for the amount of time it takes to count "one."

Notes with a stem and hollow oval head are called half notes. A half note gets two counts, or beats, per measure. It is twice as long as a quarter note, so count "one, two."

An eighth note has a solid head, a stem, and a flag. Often, two eighth notes will be connected. The eighth note lasts half as long as a quarter note. So if you are mentally counting the beats in the measure, you would count "one and two and three and four and." Each of these words would represent an eighth note; you would play on the "one" but not on the "and," for example.

A whole note is a hollow circle. It indicates a note that receives four beats.

Sometimes, you will see a dot next to a note, as shown in the lower left corner. This means that when you play the note, you need to add one-half the original value of the note to its length. For example, a dotted half note is played for three beats, while a dotted quarter note is extended by an extra eighth. (In 4/4 time each measure would have eight eighth notes; the dotted quarter note would be played for three eighths.)

Rests also appear in the measure. These symbols indicate to the musician when he or she should take a brief break from playing. Like notes, there are different symbols for rests, depending on how long the musician should be silent. Two common rests, quarter note and half note rests, are pictured below.

Dotted Half Note

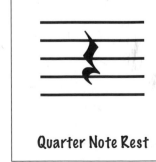

Quarter Note Rest

Half Note Rest

3. Reading Treble Clef

Specific notes are assigned to the different lines and spaces on the musical staff. The only way to be sure what note each line or space represents is to look at the beginning of the staff, where you will see a symbol called a clef. There are several different clef symbols; each indicates to the person reading the music which notes the lines and spaces on the staff represent. The most common of these is the treble, or G, clef (pictured at right). When you see the treble clef, you'll know what notes are played at each line and space.

The Treble Clef

The Lines Only

When you see the treble clef, you'll know that the note on the bottom line is E. The next line up is G, then is B, then D, then F.

To remember the order, most students use a mnemonic device like:

Every **G**ood **B**oy **D**eserves **F**udge

The Spaces

For music written in treble clef, the spaces from the bottom up are F, A, C, E.

Yes, it's the word "face," which is another mnemonic that students can use to remember the notes in the spaces.

Remember, notes can be written above and below the staff.

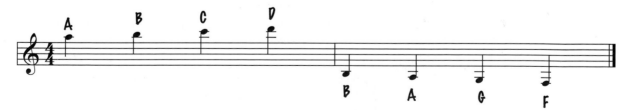

In the example above, some of the notes have an extra line or two through them, either above or below the five-line staff. These are called ledger lines, and they help the musician to easily identify the proper note.

4. Reading Bass Clef

The other clef you need to know is the bass clef, shown below. The notes on this staff are different from the ones in treble clef.

The Bass Clef

The Bass Clef Lines

The lines, from bottom to top, are G, B, D, F, and A.

A mnemonic that will help you remember this order is:

Great **B**ig **D**ogs **F**ight **A**lligators.

The Bass Clef Spaces

The spaces in bass clef are A, C, E, and G.

The phrase **A**ll **C**ows **E**at **G**rass may help you remember what notes go on which spaces.

Piano music is written in both the treble and the bass clefs. They are joined together on what is called a Grand Staff (left).

The note pictured here, one line below the treble clef, is Middle C, so called because it is in the center of the piano keyboard. Middle C is an important note; beginners can use it as a reference point for proper fingering.

It might be helpful to quiz yourself to make sure you remember the notes in each clef. Draw five lines on a sheet and try naming them as they would be in treble clef, then in bass clef. To play piano, you will have to know both and be able to read them at a glance, so learning the notes is important.

5. Time Signature

In addition to the clef symbols, there is also a time signature written at the beginning of the musical staff. The time signature tells the musician how many beats are in each measure, and which note is valued at one beat.

The top number indicates the number of beats per measure. So in 4/4 time, there are four beats per measure, while in 3/4 time there are three beats per measure. The bottom number tells which note gets one beat. A 4 on the bottom of the time signature means the quarter note gets one beat.

For another example, in 6/8 time each measure would have 6 beats and the eighth note would be played as one beat.

Below are some examples of time signatures that are often used in piano music. You will sometimes see a C in the place of a time signature. That simply stands for 4/4, or common time. Most of the music you will see will be written either in 4/4 or 3/4 time.

2/4 Time   4/4 Time
        (also known as common time)

3/4 Time   6/8 Time

6. The Sharp and Flat Symbols

The figure on the F line in this picture to the right is called a sharp. If you see it placed in front of a note, you should play the note a half step up. For example, if you see an F with the # next to it, you would not play F, you would play the note a half tone higher. This note is called F#.

On the piano, sharps are played using the black keys. An F# would be played with the black key to the right of the F key.

Notes can also be flat, which means they are played a half tone lower. A flat sign looks like a small b (pictured at left). To play a Gb, you would use the black key to the left of the G key.

As you've probably figured out, sharps and flats can indicate the same tone. The note G is one step above F, so you use the same key to play F# (a half-step up) and Gb (a half-step down). These are known as enharmonic notes.

The first place you will see flats and sharps is in the key signature. If you see one sharp in the key signature (like the image at the top right on this page) the music is in the key of G. If you see one flat in the key signature (like the staff above left) the music is in the key of F. Below are the sharps and flats that will appear in the key signatures of some other common musical keys.

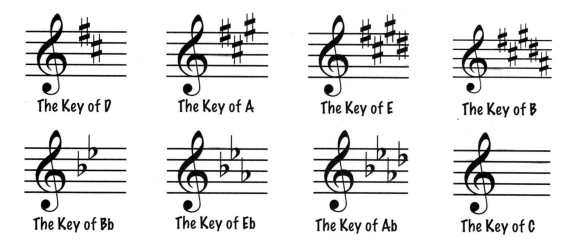

The Key of D   The Key of A   The Key of E   The Key of B

The Key of Bb   The Key of Eb   The Key of Ab   The Key of C

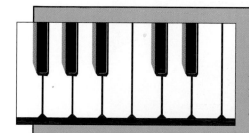

Just a Reminder

Music uses only the letters A through G to represent notes, and the notes are always in alphabetical order as they go up and down the staff.

You can tell which note should be sharp or flat depending on the line where the symbol appears in the key signature. Remember, when you see sharps or flats in the key signature, that note must be adjusted each time it is played.

Sometimes a song may include a note or notes that are not in the same key as the rest of the song. When this happens, you will see a sharp or flat symbol to the left of the note in your music. If the note is already sharp or flat, you may see another symbol next to the note. This means to play the natural tone. Musicians call these notes "accidentals." As you see from the staff below, the symbols show the musician when to start and stop playing sharps and flats.

Natural Symbol

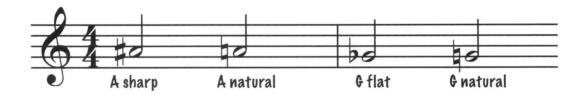

A sharp   A natural   G flat   G natural

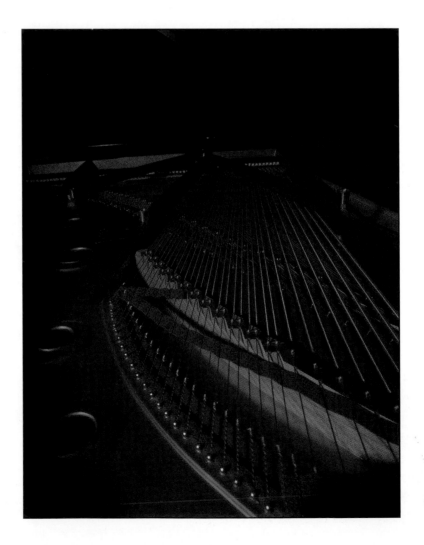

7. Finding the Notes on the Keyboard

In music different notes are represented by the letters A, B, C, D, E, F, and G. After G, the pattern starts again with A and repeats. A full-sized piano has 88 keys, so it repeats the full pattern seven times, plus four additional notes.

The keys of the piano are color-coded white and black. The black keys are arranged in groups of twos and threes. The white key that you see before any group of two black keys is C. The C that is almost in the center of the piano is called Middle C.

As you sit before the piano, find Middle C. Now find all the C notes on the piano. As you play the C notes, or any note, listen carefully to the notes you play. This will really help you tune your ear. Notice that the C at the left has a low-pitched tone and the C on the far right has a high-pitched tone. We will talk about this later.

Now that you know your C, let's move on to another note that is easy to find. The note before every set of three black keys is the note F. Again, find all of the F notes on the keyboard.

As soon as possible take time to memorize the notes on the piano. Remember there are only seven letters repeated over and over again. Try working your way up the keyboard, hitting each key from lowest to highest and saying the notes out loud as you go.

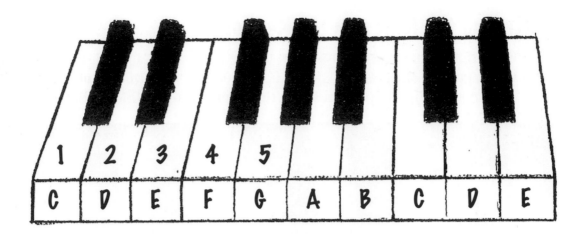

8. The Right Hand

Most music is played in the middle of the piano. This is called the middle range. And most of the time the melody of a song is played by the right hand. A melody or tune can only go in one of three ways:

1. It may ascend, or go up each line and/or space.
2. It may descend, or go down each line and/or space.
3. It may repeat, meaning it would stay on the same note.

First, you need to find the proper place for your right hand. Start by placing your thumb (finger 1, as shown in the fingering diagram below) on Middle C, as shown in the keyboard diagram above and the picture below.

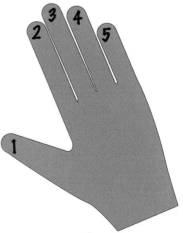

Right Hand Fingering

Next, place your index finger (finger 2) on the note D.
Place your middle finger (finger 3) on E, your ring finger (4) on F, and your pinky finger (5) on G. Make sure you play using the rounded part of your fingertips and hold your wrists parallel with the floor.

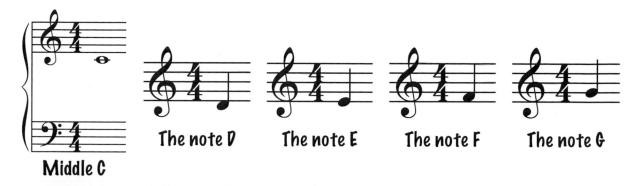

Middle C   The note D   The note E   The note F   The note G

Gently play each of the notes: first C, then D, E, F, and G. Play the pattern over and over again starting with your thumb. Keep your fingers relaxed, press firmly, and lift each finger as the next finger plays the next note.

The proper fingering is marked above the notes as they appear on the musical staff.

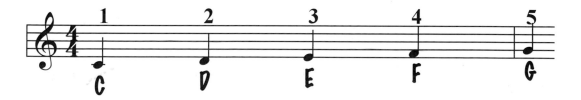

Over the next few pages, there are exercises and songs that you can use to practice. Practice these until you can play the exercises evenly and smoothly.

C through G, ascending half notes

C through G, ascending quarter notes

C through G, ascending eighth notes

C through G, ascending whole notes

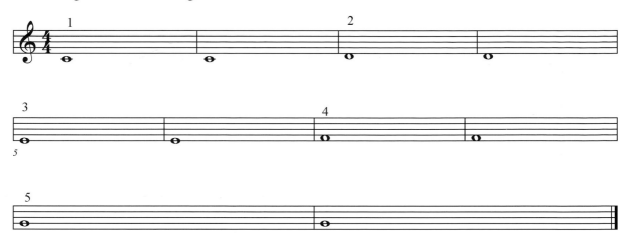

C through G, descending half notes

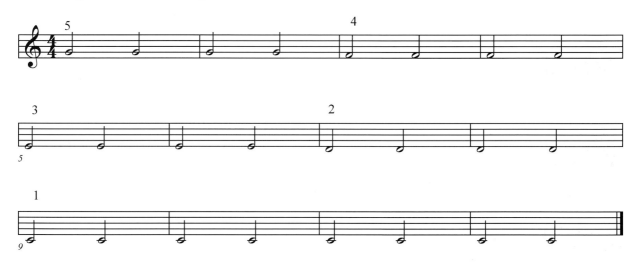

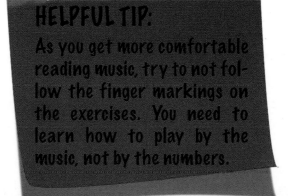

HELPFUL TIP:
As you get more comfortable reading music, try to not follow the finger markings on the exercises. You need to learn how to play by the music, not by the numbers.

C through G, descending quarter notes

C through G, descending whole notes

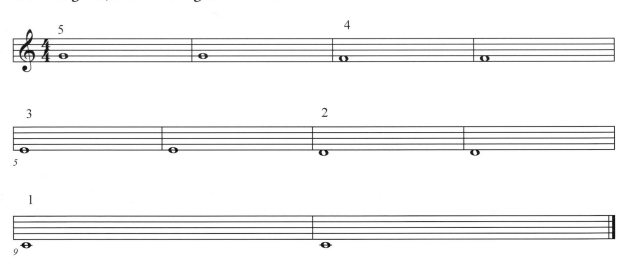

Helpful Hint

It is important to become familiar with the piano keyboard. To help you remember the notes, try labeling the keys with a bit of masking tape.

C through G, descending eighth notes

C through G, half notes

C through G, quarter notes, exercise 1

C through G, your first tune

C through G, your second tune

C through G, your third tune

C through G, up and down

C through G, quarter notes, exercise 2

C through G, half, quarter, and eighth notes, exercise 1

C through G, half, quarter, and eighth notes, exercise 2

Test What You've Learned So Far

As you play "Little Baby Sleeping" and "Go Tell Aunt Rhody" below, see if you can answer the following questions:

1. Which measures have ascending, step-wise progressions (the next note played is the next one up on the staff)?
2. Which measures have descending skip progressions (the next note played drops down more than one note)?
3. Which measures have repeated notes?
4. Where are the measures repeated?

The correct answers are at the bottom of the page. More challenging versions of these songs can be found on pages 73 and 77, respectively.

Little Baby Sleeping

Go Tell Aunt Rhody

American Folk Song

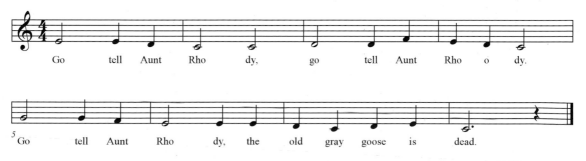

9. The Left Hand

When you're ready to take a break from practicing with your right hand, we can start working on basic fingering for the left hand. Place your left hand on the keyboard with your pinky on the C below Middle C, your ring finger on D, your middle finger on E, your index finger on F, and your thumb on G.

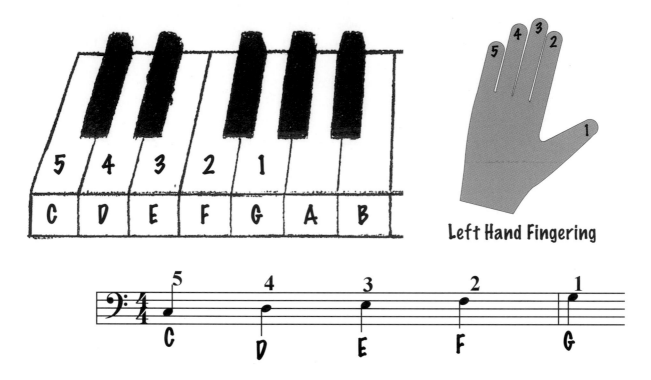

Left Hand Fingering

Gently play the notes C, D, E, F, G. Play the pattern over and over again starting with your pinky and playing C, D, E, F, and G. As you practice, always check your fingering and position. Look and see which measures have the notes going up by step, which have it going down by step, and which measures are the same.

Bass clef, C through G, ascending half notes

The note C   The note D   The note E   The note F   The note G

Bass clef, C through G, ascending quarter notes

Bass clef, C through G, ascending whole notes

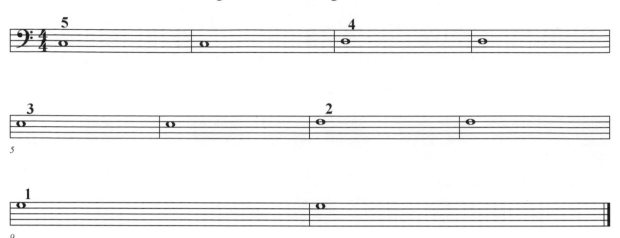

Bass clef, C through G, ascending eighth notes

Bass clef, C through G, descending half notes

Bass clef, C through G, descending quarter notes

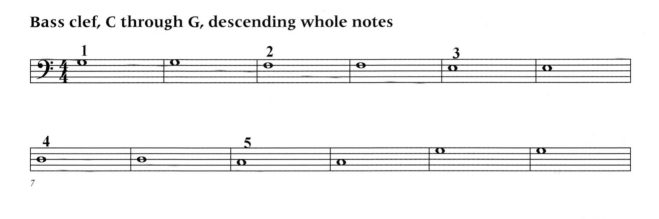

Bass clef, C through G, descending whole notes

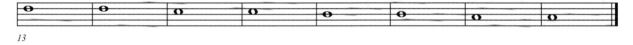

Bass clef, C through G, descending eighth notes

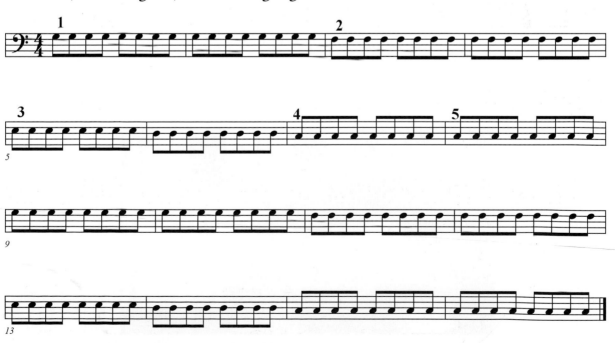

Bass clef, C through G, quarter notes

Bass clef, C through G, half, quarter, and eighth notes

10. Right and Left Hand Together

Now that you've warmed up with both hands, you're ready to try playing some songs using both hands. Place the fingers of your right and left hands in their starting places (right thumb on Middle C, left thumb on the G below Middle C).

Both hands, half note duet

Did You Know?

Franz Liszt first used the term "recital" at a concert in London in June 1840. He often played before 3,000 people and was the first solo performer to play entire programs from memory.

Playing together with quarter notes

Quarter note duet

Up and down eighth notes and half notes, exercise 1

Up and down eighth notes and half notes, exercise 2

HELPFUL TIP:
As you practice always check your fingering and position. Look to see which measures have the notes going up by step, which go down by step, and which are the same.

PART TWO

Playing Chords

After practicing those exercises, you should feel more comfortable with your fingering, and more confident in your ability to read the music. If you feel you are ready, we can move on to the next step: playing chords. A chord includes three or more notes played at the same time. Chords are essential for piano music and are usually played by the left hand.

1. The C Chord

Start by placing the pinky of your left hand on the C below Middle C, your middle finger on E, and your thumb on G. Press the three keys down at the same time. You are now playing the C chord. Because the lowest note being played in this chord is a C, this position is known as the root position.

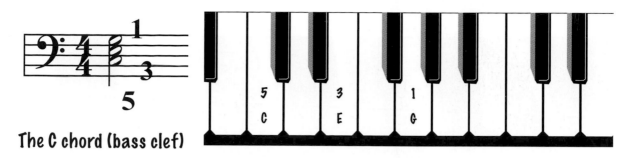

The C chord (bass clef)

The C chord is made of the notes C, E, and G. Practice playing the chord using the following exercises:

The C chord, half notes

The C chord, quarter notes

The C chord, half, quarter, and whole notes

Let's shift your left hand now. There are two other possible ways to play a C chord because the chord has three notes. The E could be the lowest note or the G could be the lowest note. These are called the first and second inversions, respectively.

To try the first inversion, place your pinky on the E below Middle C, your middle finger on G, and your thumb on Middle C. Play these three notes together. This is still a C chord, just in another position. You are still only playing the notes C, E, and G, but this time the E is the bottom note.

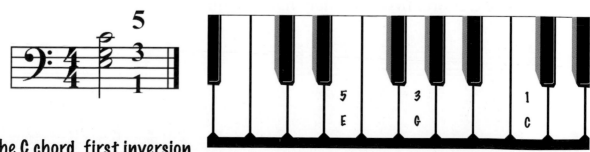

The C chord, first inversion

The fingering for the C chord, first inversion, is pictured above. Use the following exercises to practice playing this version of the chord.

The C chord, first inversion, half notes

The C chord, first inversion, quarter notes

The C chord, first inversion, half and quarter notes

In the next exercise, practice going from the root position C to the first inversion.

The C chord, root to first inversion

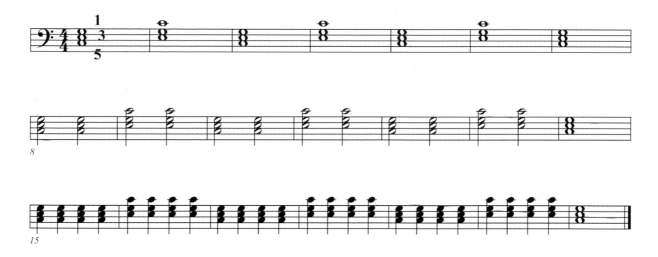

Now we'll try the second inversion. Place your pinky on G, your index finger on Middle C, and your thumb on E above Middle C. Press all the keys together and you will be playing the second inversion of the C chord.

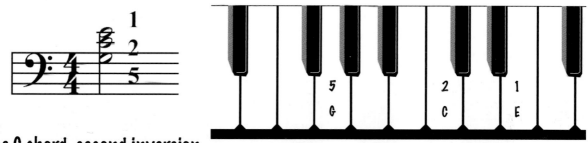

The C chord, second inversion

Following are some exercises using the second inversion of the C chord. A picture showing the proper fingering of this chord appears at the top of the next page.

The C chord, second inversion, half notes

The C chord, second inversion, quarter notes

The C chord, second inversion, whole, half, and quarter notes

2. The C Chord, Treble Clef

Next, we'll try playing chords with the right hand. Put your thumb on Middle C, your index or second finger on E above Middle C, and your ring finger or fourth finger on G, as pictured below. Play them all together. This is also a C chord.

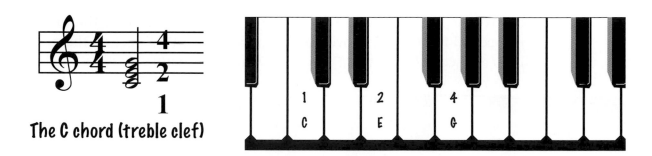

The C chord (treble clef)

Practice playing the chord using the following exercises:

The C chord, half notes

The C chord, quarter notes

The C chord, half, quarter, and whole notes

Let's shift the right hand now to the first inversion. Place your thumb on the E above Middle C, your second finger on G, and your pinky on the C above Middle C.

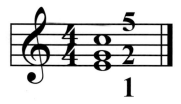

The C chord (first inversion)

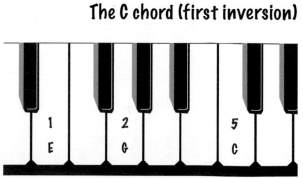

Now try the second inversion with your right hand. Place your thumb on G, your second finger on C above Middle C, and your ring finger on the next E. This is the second inversion C chord for your right hand.

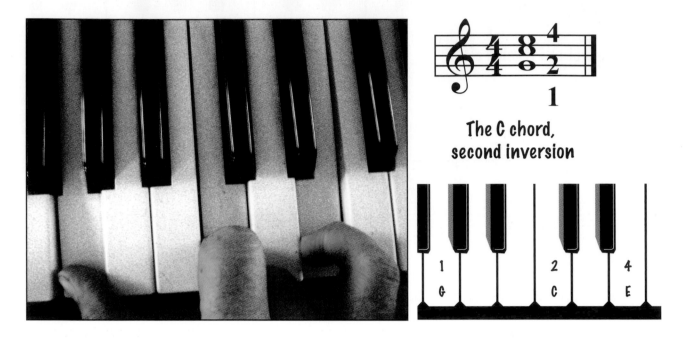

The C chord, second inversion

Practice with the following exercises.

The C chord, second inversion, half notes

The C chord, second inversion, quarter notes

The C chord, root, first, and second inversions, quarter notes

3. Using Both Hands

Now, you're ready to try playing the C chord using both hands together. In the first exercise, you'll use your right hand to play a simple melody, while playing the root C chord with your left hand. In the second exercise, you'll reverse this, using your left hand to play the melody and your right to play the chords.

Upper hand melody and C chords

Lower hand melody and C chords

In this next exercise, you'll again play the melody with your left hand, while with your right you'll play the C chord root and first inversion.

Lower hand melody and C chord inversions

4. The F Chord

The next chord you'll need to know is the F chord. To play it with your left hand, place your left pinky on the F below Middle C, your middle finger on A, and your thumb on Middle C.

The F chord

The F chord, half notes

The F chord, quarter notes

The F chord, whole, half, and quarter notes

Next is the first inversion of the F chord. Place your pinky on A below Middle C, your middle finger on Middle C, and your thumb on the F above Middle C. Practice this chord with the following exercises.

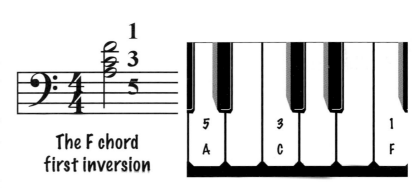

The F chord
first inversion

The F chord, first inversion, half notes

The F chord, first inversion, quarter notes

The F chord, first inversion, whole, half, and quarter notes

The F chord second inversion

Now let's shift into the second inversion. This means playing the chord with A as the low note. Still using your left hand, place your pinky on C below Middle C, your index finger on F, and your thumb on A. This is your second F chord. Use the following exercises to practice playing the chord.

The F chord, second inversion, half notes

The F chord, second inversion, quarter notes

Practice playing the chords in the root and inversion positions.

C chord, root position; F chord, second inversion

F chord, root and second inversion, half notes

F chord, root and second inversion, quarter notes

C and F chords, roots and inversions, half notes

5. The F Chord, Treble Clef

Now let's switch to using your right hand. Place your thumb on F above Middle C, your second finger on A, and your ring finger on C above Middle C.

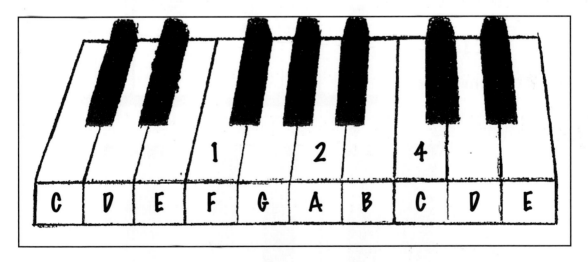

The F chord, treble clef

F chord, half notes

F chord, quarter notes

F chord, half, whole, and quarter notes

Now try the first inversion of the F chord with your right hand. Put your thumb on A above Middle C, your index finger on C above Middle C, and your pinky on the next F.

The F chord, first inversion

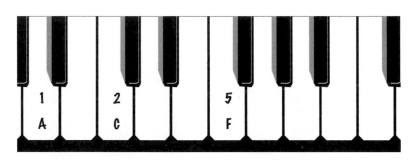

Practice this with the following exercises.

F chord, first inversion, half notes

F chord, first inversion, quarter notes

F chord, root and first inversion, half notes

Now let's move into the second inversion. Place your thumb on C, your second finger on F, and your ring finger on A.

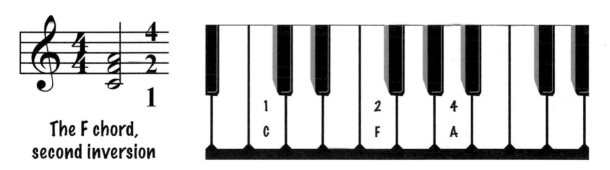

The F chord, second inversion

F chord, second inversion, half notes

F chord, second inversion, quarter notes and whole notes

F chord, whole, half, and quarter notes

Practice playing the chords in the different positions.

F chords, root and second inversion, half notes

Now practice going from one chord to another. These hand positions will be very important for you to learn, so practice switching between them often.

C chord root and F chord second inversion, half notes

Did You Know?

In 1952 American composer John Cage debuted his performance art piece "four minutes and 33 seconds." The three movements are played without sounding a single note.

6. The G Chord

The next chord we'll learn is the G chord in the bass clef. To play the chord, place your left pinky on the G below Middle C, your middle finger on B, and your thumb on D above Middle C, as pictured above.

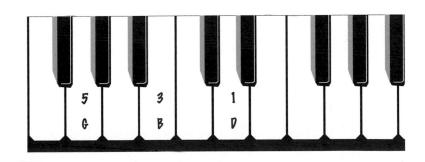

The G chord (bass clef)

G chord, whole, half, and quarter notes

G chord, half and quarter notes

Now try the first inversion of the G chord. Move your pinky to the second B below Middle C, your middle finger on the D below Middle C, and your thumb on the G below Middle C.

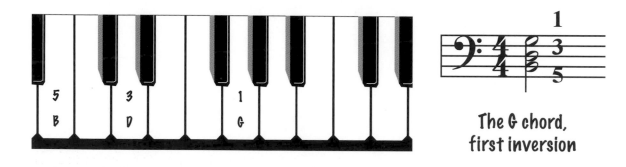

The G chord,
first inversion

Use the following lessons to practice this chord.

G chord, first inversion, half notes

G chord, first inversion, quarter notes

G chord, first inversion, whole, half and quarter notes

Now let's do the second inversion of the G chord. Still using your left hand, place your pinky on D, your index finger on G, and your thumb on B. The second inversion of the G chord can either be played starting on the D above Middle C or the D below Middle C. What makes this the second inversion is that the lowest note is a D.

The G chord, second inversion

G chord, second inversion, half notes

G chord, second inversion, half and quarter notes

Practice playing the chords in the different positions:

G chord, root and second inversion, half notes

Now try going from the C chord to the G chord:

C and G chords, whole, half, and quarter notes

C and G chords

G chord root and C chord first inversion, half notes

7. The G Chord, Treble Clef

Now try playing the G chord with your right hand. Place your thumb on G above Middle C, your second finger on B, and your ring finger on D, as shown in the illustration below.

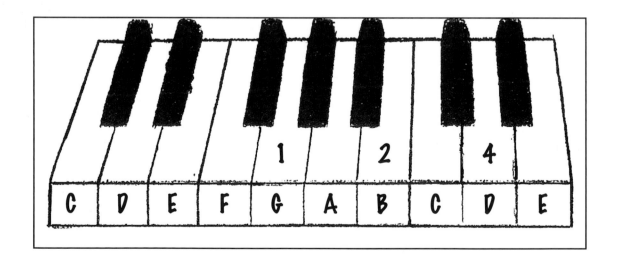

The G chord (treble clef)

G chord, root, half notes

G chord, root, quarter notes

G chord, whole, half, and quarter notes

G chord, half and quarter notes

Let's move on to the first inversion of the G chord on the right hand. Place your thumb on the B above Middle C, your index finger on High D, and your pinky on the next G, as shown below.

**The G chord
first inversion**

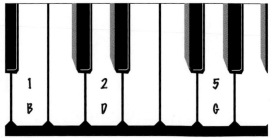

Practice with the following exercises.

G chord, first inversion, half notes

G chord, first inversion, quarter notes

G chord, root and first inversion, half notes

Now let's try the second inversion. Place your thumb on D, your index finger on G, and your ring finger on B.

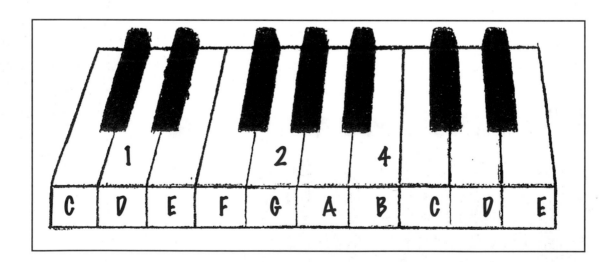

The G chord second inversion

G chord, second inversion, half notes

G chord, second inversion, quarter notes

G chord, second inversion, half and quarter notes

The great pianist, composer, and bandleader Duke Ellington (1899–1974), shown here seated at a piano, is widely considered one of the most influential American musicians of all time.

Now play the C and the G chords, paying particular attention to how these chords feel.

C and G chords, half notes, exercise 1

C and G chords, half notes, exercise 2

G chord, half and quarter notes

Now try playing this song, which requires both chords. Watch the time signature; the song is in 3/4 time, so there are three quarter notes in each measure.

Du Lac So Clear

French

Piano

Du Lac So Clear

French

8. The C Scale

Next, you'll need to learn how to play the C scale. Place the thumb of your right hand on C and play the notes C, D, and E. To play the note F, slide your thumb under your fingers and play the note F with your thumb, then G with your index finger, A with your middle finger, B with your ring finger, and C with your pinky.

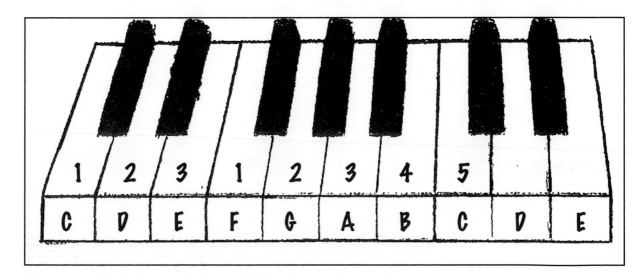

Playing the C Scale with the Right Hand

To play the C scale, start on C and play the notes C, D, and E with your thumb, first, and second fingers, respectively.

Slide your thumb under your fingers and play the note F with your thumb, then G with your index finger.

Now play the note A with your middle finger, B with your ring finger, and C with your pinky.

C scale, right hand, quarter notes

As you come back down the scale, play the high C with your pinky, B with your ring finger, A with your middle finger, G with your index finger, and F with your thumb. Slide your middle finger over the top of your thumb and play E. Play the D with your index finger and Middle C with your thumb.

C scale, right hand up and down, quarter notes

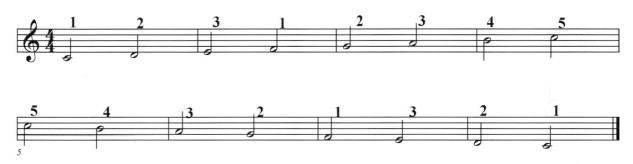

To play the C scale with your left hand, start with your pinky on C below Middle C. Play D with your ring finger, E with your middle finger, F with your index finger, and G with your thumb. Slide your middle over and play the A, your index finger the B, and your thumb the C.

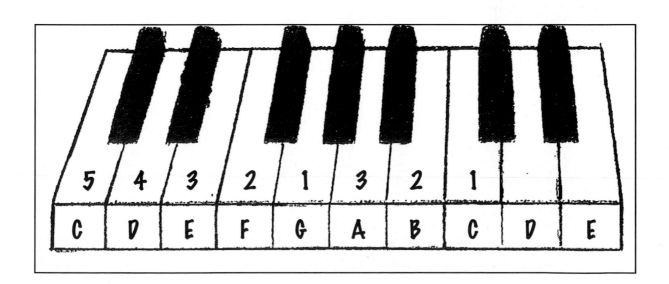

9. Scales and Other Exercises

Practice these scales as often as you can. This will help you learn to move your fingers quickly and train your ear to the C scale. Remember, watch the clef symbols!

C scale, left hand, exercise 1

C scale, left hand, exercise 2

C scale, both hands, exercise 1

Playing the C Scale with the Left Hand

To play the C scale with your left hand, start by playing the C below Middle C with your pinky, then play D with your ring finger and E with your middle finger.

Play the F with your index finger and G with your thumb, then slide your middle finger over to play the A.

Now play the note B with your index finger and C with your thumb.

C scale, both hands, exercise 2

A Simple Song

Kookaburra

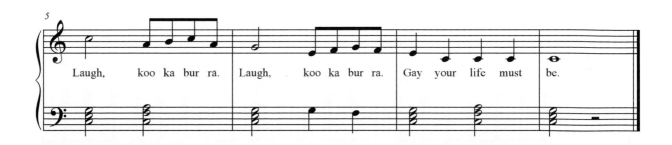

Chords and melody, exercise 1

Piano

Chords and melody, exercise 2

Piano

Fingering exercise 1

Did You Know?

Pianist Sergei Rachmaninoff, who stood six feet six inches tall, had massive hands, each of which could cover an interval on the piano of an octave plus eight semi tones.

Fingering exercise 2

10. More Chording Options

So far, with the left hand you have played a "block" type chord, meaning all the notes are played at the same time. But the left hand can be more exciting. It can break up the chord, which makes the sound a little more interesting.

As you practice the next several pieces you will see block chords in the first piece and broken chords in the second. Listen to the difference as you play.

Little Baby Sleeping

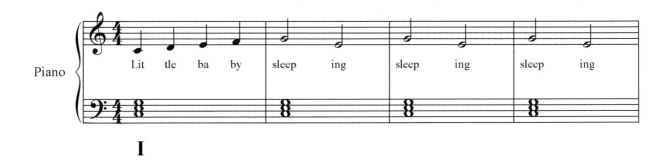

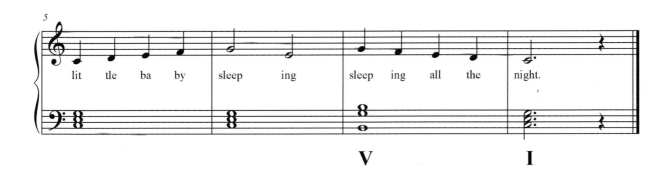

Little Baby Sleeping

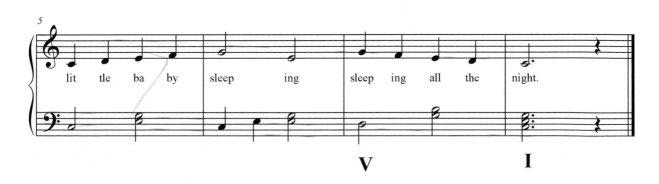

Hot Cross Buns

English nursery

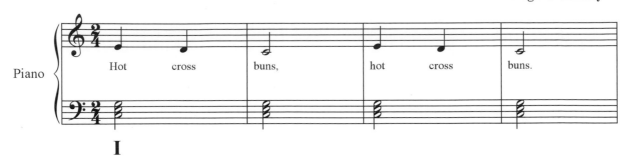

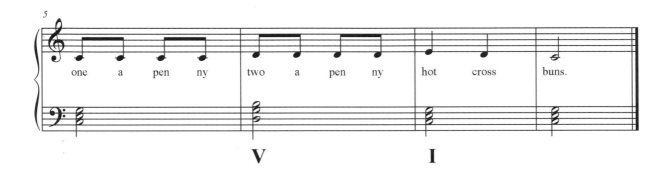

Hot Cross Buns

English nursery

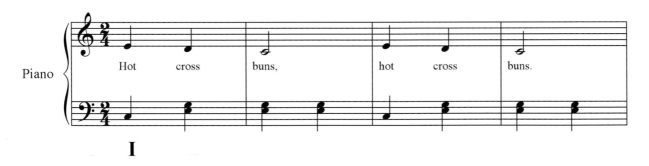

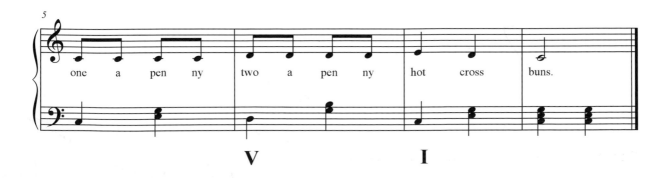

The cover of a piece of sheet music for the piano, circa 1898.

Go Tell Aunt Rhody

American Folk

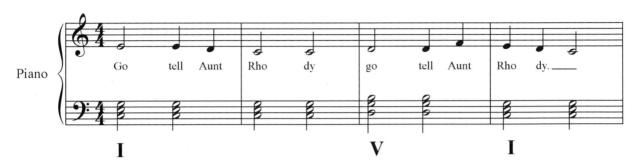

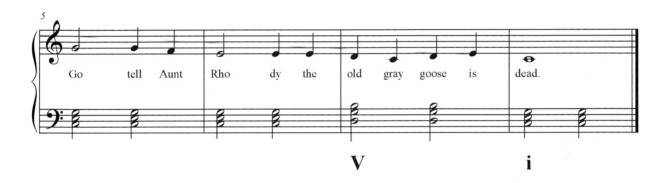

Go Tell Aunt Rhody

American Folk

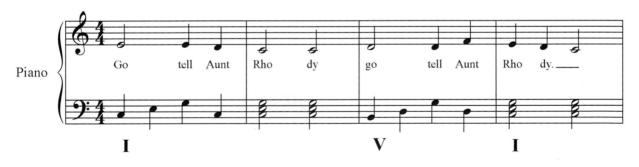

Are You Sleeping?

French

Are You Sleeping?

French

Mary Had a Little Lamb

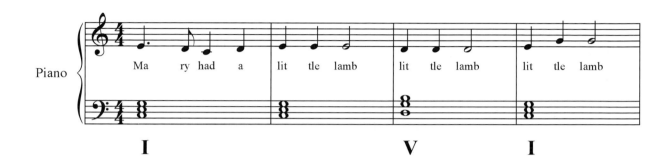

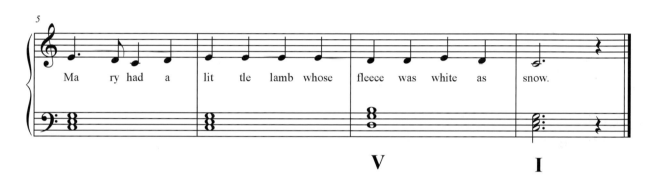

Mary Had a Little Lamb

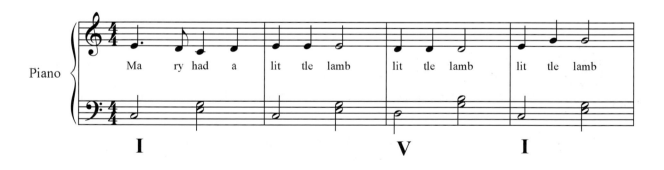

When the Saints Go Marching In

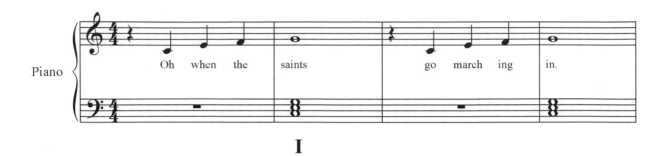

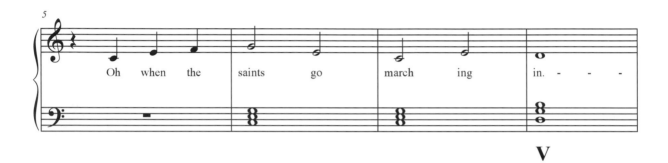

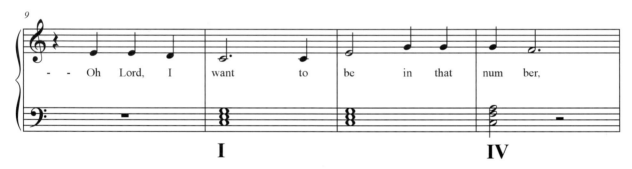

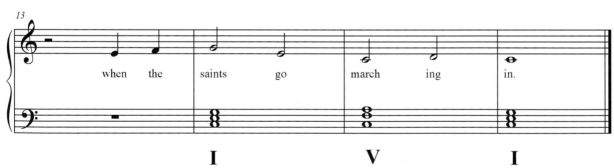

When the Saints Go Marching In

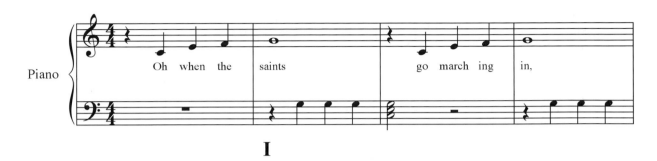

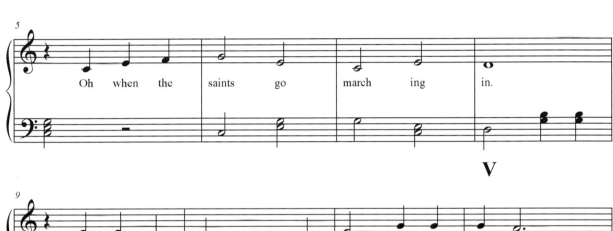

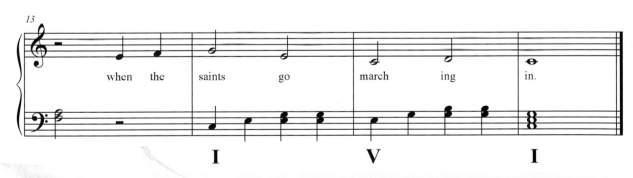

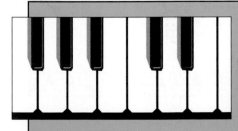

Did You Know?

The earliest version of the song "When the Saints Go Marching In" was published in 1896. By the 1920s, the song was a Dixieland jazz standard.

French Folk Song

Folk

English Folk Song

Folk

Drink to Me Only with Thine Eyes

English Folk

Piano

Drink to me on - ly wi th thine eye s and I___ will pledge with mine.

9

Or leave a kiss with in___ a cup___ and I will not want for wine.

Did You Know?

Rock 'n' Roll legend Little Richard grew up and attended church in Macon, Georgia. As he was learning to play the piano, he also tried to sing gospel music, but was turned down by some churches because he screamed the hymns.

PART THREE:

Major Chords in C

1. The I, IV, and V Chords

In some of the exercises that you have just played, you may have noticed Roman numerals beneath the music. These numerals denote certain chords that are considered important in western music. They establish what key the music is in, and contain a varying degree of tension and movement toward the root of the key.

When it appears, the I chord determines the key that a particular piece of music is written in. Thus, if the I is a C chord, the music is in the key of C. In the key of C, the F chord is the IV, and the G is called the V. Understanding this numbering is simple—look at the keyboard, and count Middle C as 1 (or I; this numeral is capitalized because it denotes a major chord), D as 2 (this would be written as a lower-case roman numeral, ii, because in the key of C, the chord is actually a D minor), E as 3 (or iii, denoting E minor), F as 4 (IV), and G as 5 (V). Hence the sequence I, IV, V.

Don't worry about the minor chords now. Instead, concentrate on practicing the three major chords in C with the right hand first.

I, IV, V chords, right hand, exercise 1

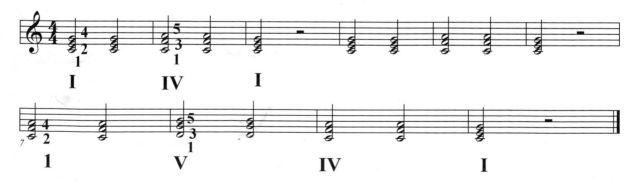

I, IV, V chords, right hand, exercise 2

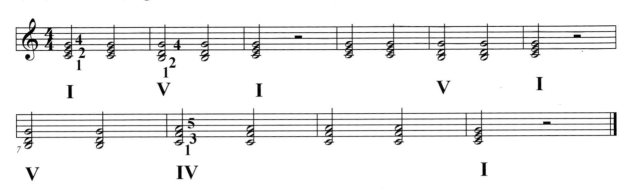

I, IV, V chords, right hand, exercise 3

Now try playing the chords with your left hand.

I, IV, V chords, left hand, exercise 1

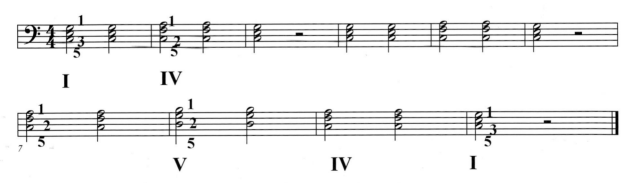

I, IV, V chords, left hand, exercise 2

I, IV, V chords, left hand, exercise 3

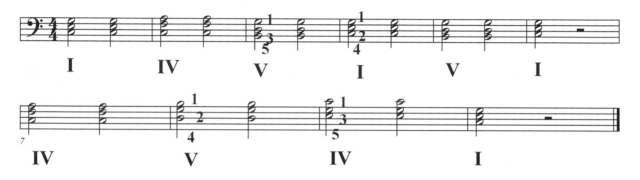

I, IV, V chords and right hand melody

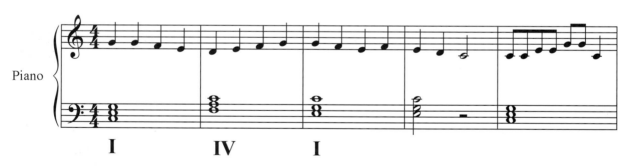

If you master these three chords and scales you will find you can play hundreds of songs, just using 3 chords. Get to know them as I, IV, and V.

I, IV, V chords, right and left hand melody

First Song in C

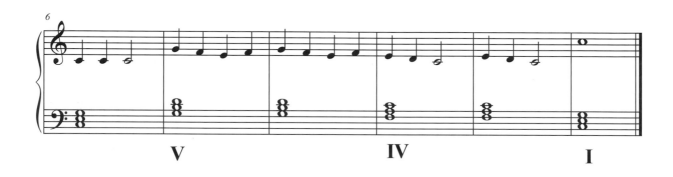

Second Song in C

Third Song in C

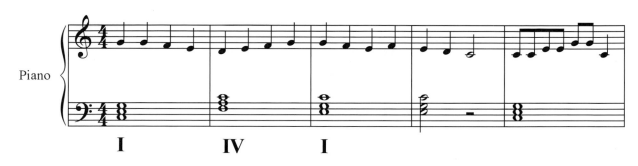

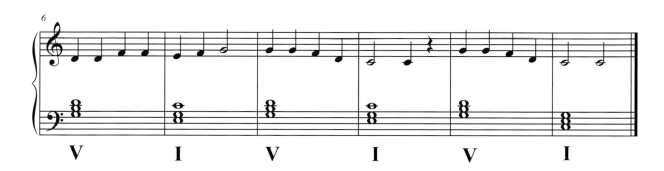

Marianna

Island song

Twinkle, Twinkle Little Star

French

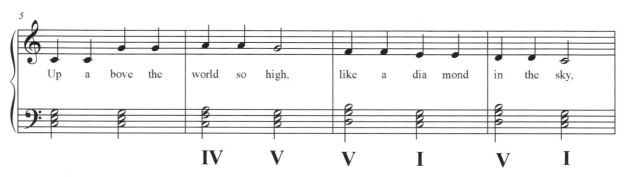

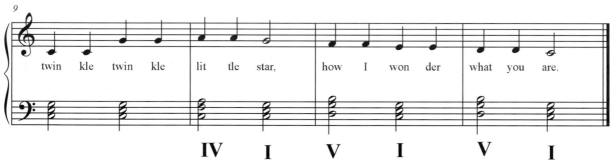

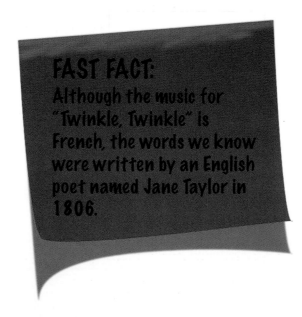

FAST FACT:
Although the music for "Twinkle, Twinkle" is French, the words we know were written by an English poet named Jane Taylor in 1806.

Twinkle, Twinkle Little Star

French

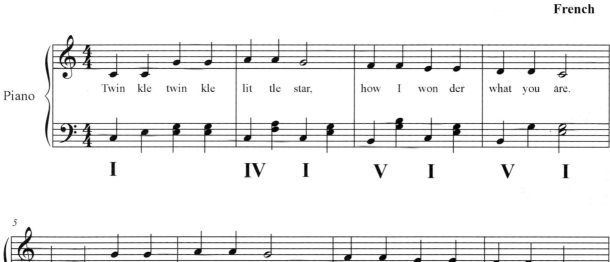

Piano

Twin kle twin kle   lit tle star,   how I won der   what you are.

I   IV   I   V   I   V   I

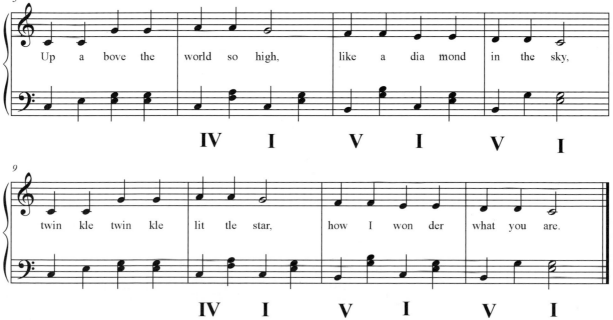

Up a bove the   world so high,   like a dia mond   in the sky,

IV   I   V   I   V   I

twin kle twin kle   lit tle star,   how I won der   what you are.

IV   I   V   I   V   I

From Symphony No. 9 Ode to Joy

Ludwig Van Beethoven

Cockles and Mussels

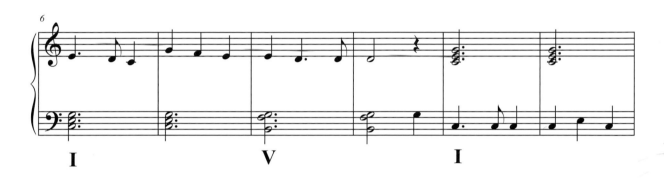

Did You Know?

Although "Cockles and Mussels" is regarded as an Irish song, it was actually written by a Scotsman, James Yorkston, and was published in London in 1884. (At that time, Ireland was still a part of the United Kingdom, which included both England and Scotland.)

Oh, Susanna

Stephen Foster

The Sea Chords 3 ways

Piano

Skip to My Lou

Folk

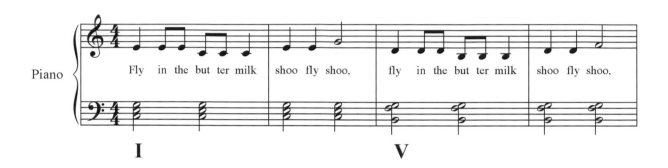

Fly in the but ter milk shoo fly shoo, fly in the but ter milk shoo fly shoo,

I   V

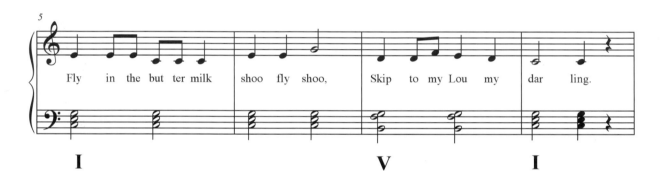

Fly in the but ter milk shoo fly shoo, Skip to my Lou my dar ling.

I   V   I

Skip, skip, skip to my Lou, Skip, skip skip to my Lou,

Skip, skip, skip to my Lou, Skip to my Lou my dar ling.

Sontina Fresesa

Piano

Hur ry hur ry run un der the big ap ple tree. Hur ry hur ry run but do not

drop any sweet jui cy ap ples. One, two, three, four, five, six, sev en.

One, two, three, four, five, six, sev en. Keep them in yo ur bas ket, do not drop the ap ples.

Did You Know?

The largest piano ever made was built by the Challen Company of London in 1935 to celebrate the Silver Jubilee of King George V. It measured eleven feet eight inches long, and its largest bass string was nine feet eleven inches long.

2. Basic Piano Care

The most important part of piano care is keeping your instrument in tune. This generally only applies to those using a real stringed piano. Tuning is best done by hiring a qualified technician. The Piano Technicians Guild (www.ptg.org) can provide a list of contacts. It is also important to remember that if you have a wooden piano, the wood and finish need to be cared for as well. They can be wiped down with a damp cloth or polished with a quality wood polish.

Protect the piano's keys by keeping the lid shut when it's not in use. If anything gets in between the keys that can't be easily removed, it is best to call a technician. You can damage the piano if you try to pry something out. A technician should also work on the insides of the piano. The strings and mechanisms can be easily damaged.

Pianos are also vulnerable to temperature and humidity. Changes in either of these can cause the piano to warp and get out of tune. Liquids of any kind inside the piano can also cause a great deal of damage. Should something spill inside, call a technician.

3. Tips for Practice

There's no definite amount of time for practicing—it's different for everyone. Generally, your practicing time should be long enough that you can do all your pieces and work on the bad spots. Your average practice session probably should not last more than 30 to 40 minutes at first.

You should start with scales and chords. Playing scales and chords can sometimes be very boring if you have lots of them to play, so make them interesting: get louder on scales going up and softer on scales going down. Try not to hit the last note too hard. Fade the last few notes out gradually. Listen carefully to make sure that your hands are exactly together if you are practicing both hands together. Slowly increase the speed over time. Keep your hands in sync. Be strong and stable. Lots can be learned by practicing technique.

Always listen to yourself when you're practicing and don't get distracted. Relax and make sure that you're not holding your breath (I know this sounds weird, but it happens). If you sense any tension, try to relax. Watch out for bad habits and try to correct them. Common ones are bending knuckles down (this one has to be practiced) and holding your fingers too high when they're not playing.

Think about how you play as well as what you play. Ask: What needs more work? What is the composer trying to say? Listen to well-known pianists on CD. You don't have to copy what they do, just listen to their different styles and techniques.

HELPFUL TIP:
Remember, practicing needs to be fun, not work. If you are frustrated with a particular exercise, just stop. Go back to a piece that you can play with confidence, and work on the difficult exercise next session.

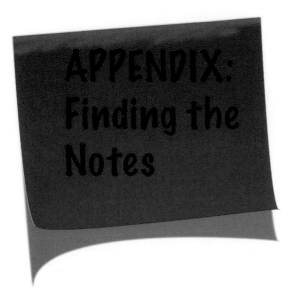

APPENDIX: Finding the Notes

Regardless of which instrument a student of music is learning, a diagram of the keys of the piano offers one of the best illustrations of how most western music is organized. Comprehending the relationship between different notes gives a pianist both a greater understanding of his or her instrument and a grasp of the basics of music theory.

Typically, a modern piano has around 88 keys. As you can see in the diagram on the opposite page, these keys are colored either black or white and repeat a specific pattern throughout the keyboard. That is, with the exception of the extreme left of the keyboard (the lowest notes) and the extreme right (the highest notes), you will find groupings of three white keys with two black keys between them and four white keys with three black keys between them. Each of these keys is given a name corresponding to the letters of the alphabet A through G. The letter names are assigned to the white, and the black keys' names are letters with either a sharp sign or flat sign after them.

The pitch that sounds when you strike the white key immediately to the left of the grouping of two black keys is known as C. Depending upon the number of keys on the piano being played, this note will reoccur six or seven times throughout the instrument. The frequency of each C is twice that of the C immediately to its left and one-half that of the C to its right. Because of this special relationship, these notes sound very similar to our ears, hence, the reason why they have the same name. The interval between these adjacent pitches with the same name is known as an octave, and this relationship is true for all similarly named notes found on the keyboard.

In order to clear up confusion caused by the fact that there are as many as 88 notes (maybe more) on a piano and many fewer note names, musicians, over time, have developed a way to differentiate between the notes that have the same name. Beginning with the C note found farthest to the left of the keyboard, a number is added to the note name indicating the octave in which the note occurs. For example, the first C that appears on the

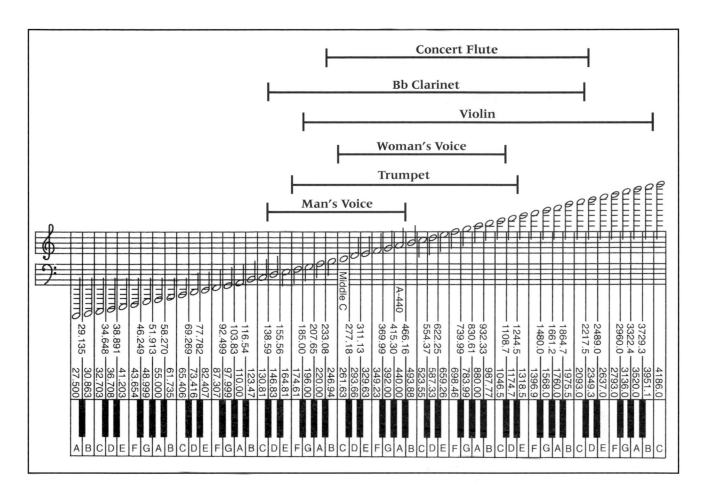

keyboard is known as "C1," the D that appears next to that is known as "D1," and so on. Middle C is also known as C4. Depending upon the piano's manufacturer, you may find that there is a different number of notes to the left of the first C on the keyboard. Since these notes do not comprise a complete octave, the number zero follows their letter name.

You'll notice that there are eleven keys between notes of the same name. Each of these keys represents a change in pitch of one half step. It can then be concluded that an octave covers a distance of 12 half steps, or six whole steps.

PIANO TIMELINE

Prehistory: Rock paintings from around 15,000 B.C. in France depict harp-like instruments. The monochord, an instrument that consisted of a single string stretched over a sound box, also dates back to early human civilization.

300 B.C.: Mention of the psaltery, which has multiple strings drawn taut across a sound box, appears in early Greek literature. The psaltery is considered the forerunner to the harpsichord, because its strings are plucked.

ca. 100 A.D.: By this time, the hammer dulcimer has been invented in Persia (modern Iran). It is considered a predecessor to the piano because it consists of multiple strings placed over a sound box, which are struck using hammers.

1150: The keyed monochord develops around this time.

1300s: The clavichord and harpsichord, two keyboard instruments that are precursors to the piano, are invented.

1598: In his letters to the Duke of Modena, Paladino describes an instrument he has developed which he calls a "Pian e Forte." Though his instrument was able to produce both soft and loud tones, it is not clear whether it is a modified harpsichord or a true hammered piano.

1700: Italian instrument designer Bartolomeo Cristofori produces his *gravicèmbalo col piano e forte* or "harpsichord with soft and loud." Dubbed the "hammer harpsichord," it features the first true escapement mechanism. All the dampers are wedge-shaped, and the small hammers are covered with leather.

1739: Domenico del Mela, assistant to Cristofori, produces the first upright piano. This instrument is more like a grand piano arranged vertically than the more compact uprights of today.

Wolfgang Amadeus Mozart   **Ludwig von Beethoven**

1745: Francisco Perez Mirabel designs a piano in which the treble notes have 3 strings per tone rather than the typical two. This allows for greater volume.

1768: Johann Christian Bach gives the first-ever piano recital in London.

1770: Ludwig van Beethoven is born. One of the first piano virtuosos, he is considered among the greatest composers of all time.

1772: The Backers Grand, manufactured in this year, has both a sustain pedal and an *una chorda* pedal. The latter pedal moves the hammer's action to one side, thereby making the piano quieter. It is the earliest known example of this type of construction.

1773: Clementi's "Sonata Opus 2" becomes one of the first pieces composed with the piano in mind instead of the harpsichord.

1770s: While Haydn's piano sonatas are popular and encourage a shift from the harpsichord to the piano around this time, Wolfgang Amadeus Mozart's piano concertos really push the instrument's popularity.

1775: Johann Behrent of Philadelphia becomes the first piano maker in America.

Library of Congress drawing of an American-made piano, circa 1803.

1791:   Mozart dies at age 35.

1800:   The first true upright piano is made by John Isaac Hawkins.

1801:   Edward Riley builds a transposing piano, in which the keyboard moves laterally, allowing different notes to be played by the keys.

1810:   Frédéric Chopin, who would become one of the most admired, influential, and prolific composers of piano music, is born in Zelazowa, Poland. Another influential pianist and composer of the early Romantic era, Robert Schumann, is also born in this year.

1811:   Franz Liszt, piano virtuoso and renowned composer, is born. Known for his great skill and showmanship with the piano, he is considered one of history's greatest pianists.

1819:   Steel wire is first used to string pianos, which allows for greater tension and volume.

1851:   Piano makers begin to replace wooden frames with stronger, sturdier iron frames.

1873:   Sergei Rachmaninoff, who would become one of the most influential pianists of the 20th century, is born in Semyonovo, Russia.

1899:   Edward Kennedy "Duke" Ellington is born. A bandleader, pianist and composer, he is regarded as one of the most important figures in American music during the 20th century.

1904:   Jazz pianist, organist, bandleader, and influential composer William "Count" Basie is born.

1917:   Scott Joplin, the most famous composer of Ragtime music, dies.

1931:   The Neo-Bechstein piano is created. It has no soundboard and is amplified using loudspeakers.

1958:   Samick Musical Instruments is established. Beginning in 1960 the company would produce uprights, and it is now known as the world's largest maker of pianos.

1960:   The Lindner Company of Ireland began making pianos with aluminum alloy welded frames. This reduced the weight to about half that of a cast frame.

1982:   Thelonious Sphere Monk, renowned pianist and founder of bebop jazz, dies.

1989:   Vladimir Horowitz dies. An American pianist of Ukrainian birth, Horowitz was known for unrivaled use of technique and tone color in his playing.

2006:   Kemble Pianos introduce their Mozart K121 model in celebration of the 250th anniversary of the composer's birth.

INTERNET RESOURCES

http://www.menc.org/

The mission of the National Association for Music Education is to "advance music education by encouraging the study and making of music by all." Go to this site for articles related to issues in music education, making a donation, and how you can become a member.

http://www.pianofinders.com/educational/shortguide.htm

At this website you'll find a list of articles full of helpful tips for buying your first piano.

http://www.8notes.com/

A great resource for all musicians, this site has piano sheet music for 259 songs available for free download, along with fingering charts, a music terms glossary, free online metronome, and links to other useful music websites.

http://www.ibreathemusic.com/

An invaluable resource for any musician, this site has forums and articles covering a wide range of music-related topics, including composition, improvisation, and ear training.

http://www.concertpitchpiano.com/PianoCareTips.html

Here you'll find information describing the regular maintenance your piano will require in order to keep it in optimum condition.

http://www.pianoworld.com/

With almost 1,000 pages, this website has forums, games, and reference materials among other helpful tools for pianists of all skill levels.

http://www.jazzreview.com/

An excellent website for everything associated with jazz. Here you'll find CD and concert reviews, interviews with numerous musicians, and dozens of jazz-related articles.

http://www.oscarpeterson.com/

Official website of Grammy Award-winning jazz pianist Oscar Peterson. With a career spanning over 50 years, Peterson has inspired dozens of musicians and is considered by many to be one of the greatest piano players of all time.

http://www.dukeellington.com/

This is a great place to learn almost anything about a man who was not only one of America's greatest pianists, but also an accomplished composer and bandleader.

http://web.telia.com/~u85420275/

Though not his official website, this Vladimir Horowitz website is fan-run and contains a complete listing of his discography and concertography, along with a listing of this brilliant classical pianist's repertoire.

Accidental—a sharp, flat, or natural note that occurs in a piece of music but is not indicated in the key signature.

Bar lines—these vertical lines mark the division between measures of music.

Beat—the pulse of the music, which is usually implied using the combination of accented and unaccented notes throughout the composition.

Chord—three or more different tones played at the same time.

Clef (bass and treble)—located on the left side of each line of music, these symbols indicate the names and pitch of the notes corresponding to their lines and spaces.

Eighth note—a note with a solid oval, a stem, and a single tail that has 1/8 the value of a whole note.

Enharmonic notes—notes that are written differently in a musical score, but have the same pitch when played on the piano (for example, F# and Gb).

Flat sign (b)—a symbol that indicates that the note following it should be lowered by one half step. This remains in effect for an entire measure, unless otherwise indicated by a natural sign.

Half note—a note with a hollow oval and stem that has 1/2 the value of a whole note.

Half step—a unit of measurement in music that is the smallest distance between two notes, either ascending or descending. An octave is divided equally into 12 half steps.

Interval—the distance in pitch between two tones, indicated using half and whole steps.

Key signature—found between the clef and time signature, it describes which notes to play with sharps or flats throughout a piece of music.

Measure—a unit of music contained between two adjacent bar lines.

Music staff—the horizontal lines and spaces between and upon which music is written.

Natural sign—a symbol which instructs that a note should not be played as a sharp or a flat.

Notes—written or printed symbols which represent the frequency and duration of tones contained in a piece of music.

Octave—a relationship between two pitches where one tone has double (or half) the frequency of the other.

Pitch—the perceived highness or lowness of a sound or tone.

Quarter note—a note with a solid oval and a stem that is played for 1/4 of the duration of a whole note.

Repeat sign—a pair of vertical dots that appear near bar lines that indicate a section of music that is to be played more than once.

Rest—a figure that is used to denote silence for a given duration in a piece of music.

Scale—a sequence of notes in order of pitch in ascending or descending order.

Sharp sign (#)—this symbol indicates that the note following it should be raised by one half-step. This remains in effect for an entire measure, unless otherwise indicated by a natural sign.

Tempo—the speed at which music is to be played. It is notated by either a word describing the relative speed of the piece or by the number of beats per minute (B.P.M.) that occur as it is played.

Time signature—located to the right of the clef and key signatures, the top digit indicates the number of beats per measure, and the number at the bottom shows which kind of note receives one beat.

Tone—a distinct musical sound which can be produced by a voice or instrument.

Whole note—a note indicated by a hollow oval without a stem. It has the longest time value and represents a length of 4 beats when written in 4/4 time.

Whole step—a unit of measurement in music that is equal to two half steps.

INDEX

ABOUT THE AUTHOR

Frank Cappelli is a warm, engaging artist, who possesses the special ability to transform the simple things of life into a wonderful musical experience. He has had an impressive career since receiving a B.A. in music education from West Chester State College (now West Chester University). Frank has performed his music at many American venues—from Disney World in Florida to Knott's Berry Farm in California—as well as in Ireland, Spain, France, and Italy. He has also performed with the Detroit Symphony, the Buffalo Philharmonic, the Pittsburgh Symphony, and the Chattanooga Symphony.

In 1987, Frank created Peanut Heaven, a record label for children. The following year, he worked with WTAE-TV in Pittsburgh to develop *Cappelli and Company*, an award winning children's television variety show. The weekly program premiered in 1989, and is now internationally syndicated.

In 1989, Frank signed a contract with A&M Records, which released his four albums for children (*Look Both Ways, You Wanna Be a Duck?, On Vacation,* and *Good*) later that year. *Pass the Coconut* was released by A&M in 1991. *Take a Seat* was released in September of 1993. With the 1990 A&M Video release of *All Aboard the Train and Other Favorites* and *Slap Me Five*, Cappelli's popular television program first became available to kids nationwide. Both videos have received high marks from a number of national publications, including *People Magazine, Video Insider, Billboard, USA Today, Entertainment Weekly* and *TV Guide*.

Frank has received many awards, including the Parent's Choice Gold Award, regional Emmy Awards, the Gabriel Award for Outstanding Achievement in Children's Programming, and the Achievement in Children's Television Award. He is a three-time recipient of the Pennsylvania Association of Broadcasters' award for Best Children's Program in Pennsylvania.